Heaven Is Like...

(What God Says About Heaven . . .)

~ I Am ~

All Bible Quotations are from the King James Version of the Bible, also known as the Authorized version.

ISBN: 978-0-9945201-8-0 (Paperback)

ISBN: 978-0-9945201-1-1 (ebook)

Library of Congress Control Number: 2021933408

Cover design by: @ArtbyAEllis

Book Design & Layout by: @ArtbyAEllis

First Edition 2021, USA

Obtenebrix Family Trust, USA

www.artbyaellis.com

Instagram: @artbyaellis

WHY DO WE CARE?

Everyone who has heard of heaven wonders what it is like there. That realm where angels and dead saints sit around on clouds all day playing harps and wishing for their wings, right? Wrong.

What about God? Is he there? What does He do there? What is everyone else doing there, why, and how do we know? Does anyone ever get bored there? Why or why not? How do we know?

It is perfectly natural to wonder about God, who He is, what He wants, and why. It is also natural to wonder what Heaven, God's home, is like. After all, how do we know we want to go there unless we first have some idea of what to expect when we get there. Strange enough, those who should know the most about this place, often seem to know no more than anyone else, and often know the least about it. Most modern Christians have no idea what Heaven is like or what to expect and themselves rely on pop culture's fictions.

So why do *you* want to go there? Or do you...

Christians may forget (and others may forget that Christians remain human, with the same weaknesses and foibles of all mankind), but God tells us a lot about His home as well as what to expect and look forward to there. Becoming a Christian means a lot more than being saved from and escaping Hell, which God calls the everlasting lake of fire, among other terms, very likely an open pit on display for all eternity, for everyone to see where those within are continually consumed by undying worms and unquenchable fire that will devour them continually, forever. See for example Isaiah 66:24, which says, "...look upon the carcasses of the men who have transgressed against me: for their worm shall not die, neither shall their fire be quenched." The Lord Himself repeats this warning in Matthew 9: 43-44. Other passages with descriptions of Hell include Revelation 20:10,15 & 21:8.

But we are more interested in Heaven, so let's set Hell aside and look at what God tells us to expect to understand about the everlasting life there that He offers to us.

Please remember as we progress through this study that while there is no single catch all passage about what Heaven is like, there truly is a great deal of information about it available to each and every one of us. Where? In God's Bible, where else? Which version of the Bible you ask? That discussion is an entire study of its own.

For now, for this study, we're going to stick to the very basics of exploring the marvelous world that awaits some of us after our bodies die and our soul and spirit depart. For this study, all quotations are from the King James Version.

Someone I know once said, "It's not the dying part that I'm afraid of. It's the getting there part that terrifies me." Now, "terrify" is a pretty strong word, but otherwise I agree. At it's very best, this life isn't even a pale shadow of what God promises we have to look forward to in Heaven, or what he originally designed for us. It's not even fair to call this planet a ruined far-flung outpost of heaven. Not anymore. Not even close. Yet most of mankind is stuck, focused on their bitter struggle for crumbs of creature comforts here, afraid to leave this life and move on to their final reward. Doubt and fears assail them as to what comes next. These fears pervade all of society. I've seen this fear and doubt in the eyes of the dying countless times, even in Christians, afraid to go home at the end, when they are at Heaven's very doorstep. That is not how our life is supposed to end. Especially not for anyone who believes they will go to Heaven when they die.

Still, a lot of us get caught up in the act of dying itself. A lot can go wrong along the way and drag the process out in painful and inconvenient ways. That is still no excuse for the desperate clinging to the last shreds of this life, trying to hang on to our failing physical body with whatever pain and suffering we're going through right before we gasp out that final breath. All we have to do is let go and everything changes for the better.

Or does it?

All of us *should* look forward to "going home," joining God, along with everyone and everything else awaiting us in Heaven. The Bible tells us how God wants us to view the death of our current body: "...whilst we are at home in the body, we are absent from the Lord...we are confident, *I say*, and willing rather to be absent from the body, and to be present with the Lord" (II Cor. 5:6,8). That is how each of us *should* look at death: Going Home At Last, leaving behind this cursed, ruined, and failing planet to join our loved ones forever in an environment that exists as God intended, uncorrupted by sin and evil, *perfect* in every way.

When we die, we "absent," or vacate, our current physical body. We depart from it. We leave it behind. This body should not be our defining characteristic. It is temporary. This doesn't mean we shouldn't take care of it. But our soul and spirit, the essence of who we are separates from this body and continues on. They remain, and we become "present with the Lord" and reside where God Himself dwells, in Heaven. We might not even be aware of the journey, it happens so fast. We do have a hint as to how we get there, from Luke 16:22: "And it came to pass, that the beggar died, and was carried by the angels."

The apostle Paul shares with us his own experience with the death of his body in Second Corinthians chapter 12: "I knew a man in Christ about 14 years ago, (whether in the body, I cannot tell; or whether out of the body I cannot tell: God knoweth) such an one CAUGHT UP TO THE THIRD HEAVEN" (II Cor. 12:2). Paul is talking about himself here. Note how he says he was caught up to the third heaven. God's heaven, home, and present abode. What most of us think of when we speak of "Heaven." What are the first two heavens? They are the heavens of Genesis chapter one, where God created and divided them from each other during creation. They're referred to in the Bible as "firmaments." The firmament of heaven, where hang the sun, moon, stars, and planets, and the "open firmament," in which birds fly "above the earth." The Earth was formed and placed into the first of these and the second became our atmosphere. This "third heaven" then is another place beyond the stars of outer space, another realm beyond the confines of the heavens and earth created a Genesis. Remember this the next time some supposed guru claims to pinpoint the location of God's Heaven, the apostle Paul's third heaven, within the night sky above. They're ignoring what God himself says, that His heaven already existed before the dawn of creation of the entire universe that we know and can perceive from planet Earth. As did the angels, who witnessed and understood God's work of creation recounted in Genesis. Job chapter thirty-seven touches on this fact in verse seven when it refers to the "morning stars," or angelic rulers, and the "sons of God" already in existence before mankind's creation, before the events of Genesis 1:2, that they witnessed, when the Spirit of God was seen by them to move about above the waters that then covered all the surface of this planet. This pre-existing "third heaven," what we will see and experience when we arrive there, and what those there now are experiencing is our focus of this study.

We can't see it and we can't experience it yet. What we do have are dim glimpses, shadows in a dark mirror, snapshots of small pieces of heaven that hint at the greater whole. It's these same static snapshots, combined with satan's program of misinformation to mankind that often leaves even Christians thinking that Heaven is or will be a dull or static existence, a perpetual ennui where no one ever ages matures or changes. Nothing could be further from the truth. Even now, Heaven is a *very* active environment. God, our Father, is there on his throne at least some of the time, with our Lord Jesus

Christ, His son, sitting at his right hand for the time being. There are angels and other creatures in attendance in his throne room as well. These facts are most apparent within the Bible books of Isaiah, Ezekiel, & Revelation, but many other passages corroborate them. Even for most Christians, this snapshot is the extent of their knowledge of heaven and its environment outside of modern or Renaissance art and pop culture.

So what is outside that throne room? What is everybody doing there? Does God just sit there all the time? Do angels have wings? Will we? Does anyone sit around strumming harps? What do entertainment, jobs, organization, sports, or technology look like in Heaven? God is not silent about any of this, so what does he say?

GOD's DESIGN:

A PLAN FOR HEAVEN & EARTH

Always start at the beginning if you can. It's the best place to begin. Where does that take those of us born long millennia afterwards? Here, of course, planet Earth. Surprising as it may sound, this earth is where God designed and intended His home to be. That tells us an incredible amount right there. God didn't plan to live in the frustrating wasteland that comprises most of earth today. God had a specific plan for the Earth. He still does. Let's take a peek at what He says His plan is and how that helps us relate to and understand God's Heaven, now and in the future.

When God created the earth, He very deliberately replicated much of what He has in mind in His third heaven and placed it on this planet. While God resides in Heaven now, He created the Earth to be His dwelling place amidst His creation. This is why He created on Earth many of the same environments and surroundings He was accustomed to existing around Him in heaven. He took many of the best and most favorite features already familiar to the angelic beings in His retinue. This way, they too will feel right at home with familiar surroundings. Not unlike those of us wealthy and fortunate enough to enjoy a separate summer or vacation home might still surround that home with favorite plants or flowers from our first home.

The angels saw God creating, fashioning, & shaping the earth much like a potter shapes clay. They knew He was duplicating Heaven on this one special planet He had chosen. God was making home suitable and comfortable for Him, and them, to dwell in the centerpiece of His entire Genesis creation, our entire known universe. This is the reason Earth is the key to our comprehension and understanding of God's heaven. God Himself draws repeated parallels throughout the Bible to help us understand. Which brings us to our next key point: how do we interpret what God tells us?

There are two main schools of thought on how to interpret what God says in the Bible. The first is that God says what He means and means what He says, The literal interpretation of God's Word. The second is that God uses "language of accommodation," that God doesn't expect us to understand what He says and take it literally so He describes heavenly concepts beyond our frame of reference, things we have no chance of understanding here on Earth, by drawing comparisons to things that we do know and understand, even though we still won't have the full and accurate picture. In other words, we are meant to imagine something similar, not to take God's descriptions as written.

Many people choose to believe God only does one or the other and rejects the other of these approaches. God, however, uses both throughout the Bible. Much of what He says and describes is quite literal, direct, and to the point as stated. When He uses language of accommodation to draw a comparison, that too is obvious. He uses clear figures of speech, "like" or "as" to make the comparison, what we call simile in English. If God doesn't draw a parallel, He intends to be taken literally, and so we shall where appropriate in this study of heaven.

Here are examples of each of these types of descriptions. In the first part of Genesis, God describes what He did when He created our heavens and earth. "And the earth was without form, and void, and darkness *was* upon the face of the deep. And the Spirit of God moved on the face of the waters" (Gen. 1:2). From that verse alone, we don't know exactly what God was *doing* when He "moved upon the face of the waters." But the angels saw and they knew. Other passages make this fact clear. We know from Job that the angels were there: " When the morning stars sang together and all the sons of God shouted for joy" (Job 38:7).

All the angelic creation, rulers and commoners alike, saw what God was doing with the earth and rejoiced, celebrated His work. They "shouted for joy" because they knew that in the middle of everything else He'd made, God was creating a very special place. A place like nowhere else in his entire Genesis creation. They saw Him create it, fashion it, mold it, and build on it. He constructed the earth much as we design and construct a building. He drew up specific plans for what He wanted to build. See again in Job: "Where wast thou when I laid the foundations of the earth? declare, if thou hast understanding. Who hath laid the measures thereof, if thou knowest? Or who hath stretched the line upon it? Whereupon are the foundations thereof fastened? or who laid the cornerstone thereof" (Job 38:4-6). Note that nowhere in this passage does God draw a comparison. God says He did these things.

Job isn't the only one He told. Hundreds of years later, we have another description of God's creation of the earth and what He was doing when He was seen first creating, and then moving upon its waters: "Bless the Lord, O my soul, O Lord my God, thou art very great; thou art clothed with honor and majesty. Who covereth *thyself* with light as with a garment: who stretchest out the heavens like a curtain: Who layest the beams of His chambers in the waters" (Ps. 104:1-3). Here, He uses both literal descriptions of what He did and also makes some interesting comparisons. He also declares part of His purpose in fashioning this very creation: to surround Himself with honor and majesty. He set the beams, the foundation of the building He declares to be his own, somewhere in the waters that covered the entire planet at that time. Again, literal language.

But that is not all. We also have some of that figurative language we discussed earlier in this same psalm: "who coverest thyself with light AS with a garment," and "who stretchest the heavens LIKE a curtain." Both of these are meant to convey specific ideas beyond our earthly understanding and experience. What does a curtain do? It hides or conceals. What is it the celestial heavens are meant to conceal, and from whom? That passage doesn't say, but there are others on that same topic. These figurative descriptions are side by side in the same passage with literal descriptions of what God did when He formed and shaped the earth with all of the angelic realm watching Him. Remember, this satan is an angelic creature of the highest order, a cherub. Originally named Lucifer, son of the dawn, a morning star, and one of the angel's elite ruling class.

Satan saw and knew what God was doing, all before mankind existed: building God's own dwelling, a "house" with chambers, separate and distinct rooms, yet to be placed or built here on Earth. We saw that God has already prepared and laid a foundation for this building in a very particular spot on Earth. From other scriptures, we know that God even tells us at great length whereabouts these foundations could be found if we knew exactly what to look for because He tells us where on earth He will finish erecting His home on earth.

What seems impossible now is still possible for God. The psalm we looked at is all about God's greatness and majesty, a reminder that He *will* bring His very kingdom, city, and throne down to earth as He promised long ago. He hasn't abandoned any part of His plan for the earth. He will finish what He began millennia ago: bring Heaven down to Earth.

God will eventually rule all of His creation from right here on planet Earth. Numerous passages go into great detail about God's house, the location of its "foundation beams," when God covered them and why, when He will uncover them, when He will set His house on that foundation, and a whole lot more information. Enough to fill several of these studies. For this study, let us consider when God confirmed his covenanted promise to Abraham with Abraham's grandson, Jacob.

Jacob was given a dream from God: "And he dreamed, and behold a ladder set up on the earth, and the top of it reached to heaven: and behold, the angels of God ascending and descending on it. And, behold, the Lord stood above it, and said, I *am* the Lord God of Abraham thy father, and the God of Isaac: the land whereon thou liest, to thee will I give it, and to thy seed" (Gen. 20:12-13).

God not only confirmed His original Abrahamic covenant's promise to Jacob, He educated Jacob why he made such a promise in the first place. Jacob slept in the very land God would reside in, the very place God would raise His house to be the epicenter of all creation. Jacob said as much when he realized that land was "the house of God": "and Jacob awaked out of his sleep, and he said, Surely the Lord is in this place; and I knew *it* not. And he was afraid, and said, how dreadful is this place! This is none other but the house of God and this *is* the gate of heaven" (Genesis 26:16-17). This observation is confirmed in Revelation: "Behold, the tabernacle of God *is* with men, and he will dwell with them, and they shall be his people, and God himself shall be with them, *and be* their God" (Rev.21:3), which had been foretold long before in Psalms 68:18.

In Jacob's day, the city's gate was the seat of government. There, the elders of a city, its rulers, met and discussed city business and meted out justice on matters brought before them, much as our courts do today. Jacob's reference to "the gate of heaven" not only recognized that angels would come and go from that location about their, and God's, business but that it was where God would conduct heaven's official business. It will be God's seat of government. He will set His throne as well as His house in that place, which is why Jacob goes on to call that site "Beth-El," "house of God" in English. All of which tells us this earth is no mere celestial rock that randomly grew diverse life forms. It is a very special place carefully designed, crafted, and cultivated by God, the most valuable piece of real estate in all of creation.

Enter satan and his motives: jealousy and ambition to first rival and later usurp the Most High. This is also why satan worked so hard to wrest control of the Earth from mankind, to whom God had entrusted & given this planet to cultivate it. Satan recognizes its value and desires to possess it as his own, to take God's own house and home and put it to satan's own use instead, thereby making a cosmic statement of God's impotence and powerlessness before all of creation, a token proof of satan's supposed superiority over God. One part of satan's long reaching plan of evil and goal of setting thrones of his own above each of God's.

If we understand these things about God's design and plans for this planet, it makes more sense why of all the myriad planets God created throughout the universe, this Earth is and remains unique in ways we can see, sense, and understand here and now, and why it would and should have features similar to those in God's third heaven. God modeled his new home, Earth, after his current home, Heaven (Ps. 33:13-14). He made it of many of the same materials and gave it similar features such that its appearance would resemble His original dwelling place. All the more natural for His angelic attendants to transition from one home to the other in comfort. To see if this theory holds up, let's take a closer look at what God says He'll place on those foundation beams He laid when He created and crafted the earth so long ago.

The "chambers" are the building structures of a massive city unlike any other. A city God crafted in heaven and will bring down to earth in a time yet to come. This city is part of God's promises to Israel when God's personal focus and attention on mankind will return to them after our current age, the dispensation of gentile grace, ends. This concept is found in the book of Hebrews with the very real physical city Abraham believed God had promised him and his descendants: "for he [that's Abraham] looked for a city which hath foundations, whose builder and maker is God" (Heb.11:10).

Note once again the reference to "foundations," referring all the way back to the Genesis creation. Abraham knew about the foundations, where they had been laid, and why. There was no confusion or misunderstanding on Abraham's part. God had told Abraham what He had done at creation, perhaps during one of His visits to Abraham, such as that recorded in Genesis chapter 18, just as He had told Abraham the purpose in God's special treatment of the Earth at creation. The "heavenly Jerusalem" foretold in Revelation is the very same city God promised and Abraham anticipated, expected, and looked forward to as he roamed "to and fro" in the land God told Abraham to take possession of as it was promised thenceforth to Abraham and his descendants forever. The very same land Israel and its neighbors continue to squabble and fight over today. A city John states in Revelation will be brought down from heaven, a grandiose city of unearthly size and dimensions made of many of the same materials we have, know, and recognize here on Earth, then and today. In John's own words: "the building of the wall of it was of jasper: and the city *was* pure gold, like unto clear glass. And the foundations of the wall of the city were garnished with all manner of precious stones. The first foundation *was* jasper; the second, sapphire; the third, a chalcedony; the fourth, an emerald; the fifth, sardonyx; the sixth, sardius; the seventh, chrysolyte; the eighth, beryl; the ninth, a topaz; the tenth, a chrysoprasus; the eleventh, a jacinth; the twelfth, an amethyst; and the twelve gates *were* 12 pearls; every several gate was of one pearl: and the street of the city *was* pure gold, as it were transparent glass" (Rev. 21:18-21).

All materials we have and know on Earth, assembled and built by God in heaven, brought down to earth whole. It follows that all these materials exists in God's third heaven, where God will bring it down from (see Rev.21:2). They existed in heaven before they were created on earth. God made this planet to resemble heavenly materials and features so that his city is not in a totally alien environment when He brings it down to earth. It will fit and blend with its surroundings. That is not all. There is plenty of other evidence God's heaven bears a close resemblance to our Earth aside from the construction and arrival of this city on Earth.

Earth-like animals, plants, food, technology, even clothing are all evidenced in heaven. The Bible scene many people are familiar with, God's throne room in heaven, displays many of these features, related by the apostle John: "round about the throne were four and twenty seats: and upon the seats I saw four and twenty elders sitting, clothed in white raiment; and they had on their heads crowns of gold. And out of the throne proceeded lightnings and thunderings and voices: *there were* seven lamps of fire burning before the throne, which are the seven Spirits of God. And before the throne *there was* a sea of glass like unto crystal: and in the midst of the throne, and round about the throne, *were* four beasts full of eyes before and behind. And the first beast *was* like a lion, and the second beast like a calf, and the third beast had a face as a man, and the fourth beast *was* like a flying eagle. And the four beasts had each of them six wings about *him*; and *they were* full of eyes within: and they rest not day and night" (Rev.4:4-8).

John speaks of elders on "seats," "crowns of gold," "lightnings and thunderings," "lamps of fire," "burning," and a sea of "glass like unto crystal" set before God's throne. All common enough and familiar on Earth, present and manifest in heaven, all described in literal language. Actual objects John witnessed in heaven. John entered God's throne room through a recognizable "door." There was a controlled atmosphere that allowed whatever substance fueled the lamps to burn. Gold and glass are shaped and used there. All very much like we might find such things on Earth, even today. What we don't find on this planet are the cherubim, the "four beasts" John witnesses, different from anything we know on Earth, though their appearance is similar in some ways to everyday creatures we know and have that must each hold a significance to God: lion, calf, man, and eagle. Clearly God already had them in some form in heaven before he created and set them here on Earth.

God speaks to us of other animals in heaven. Angelic horses are often mentioned. There must be a lot of them, and they must be of particular value there since Christ will ride a "white horse" from heaven when he returns to the earth itself at the end of the Great Tribulation. With him when he comes will be the angelic armies also riding "upon white horses" (Rev.19:14).

Armies of angels, and their horses, are mentioned in several places. Satan tempted Christ atop the temple with a reminder that the scripture promised him personal protection from "legions" of angels. A legion was the largest single unit in the Roman army at that time, consisted of upwards of six thousand soldiers, and was often an entire army unto itself. And many of these legions worth of angelic soldiers were on standby to safeguard and protect Christ if ordered. The entire angelic army in heaven awaits action orders today. We know from Revelation nine verse 16 that this angelic army numbers at least two hundred million soldiers.

The prophets Elijah and Elisha both saw portions of these armies and their horses, and recorded the experiences: "behold, *there* appeared a chariot of fire, and parted them both asunder; and Elijah went up by a whirlwind into heaven. And Elisha saw it, and he cried, My father, my father, the chariot of Israel, and the horsemen thereof" (II Kings 2:11-12). This wasn't the only time Elijah speaks about these horses or the armies that ride them. "And Elijah prayed, and said, Lord, I pray thee, open his eyes, that he may see. And the Lord opened the eyes of the young man; and he saw: and, behold, the mountain *was* full of horses and chariots of fire round about Elisha" (II Kings 6:17). No ordinary horse we know of would require divine intervention before we could see it with our own eyes. These are angelic horses from heaven, no breed we cultivate here on Earth. God has horses in heaven, similar to our horses here on this planet.

There are abundant other animals in heaven. These include creatures or versions of them that are now extinct here on Earth. For example, unicorns, found, among other places, in Job 39:10, which God brings down to earth again, from heaven, when Christ returns to rule on Earth as God declares in Isaiah 34:17. Note also the first line of Revelations 5:13: "And every creature which is in heaven...." Other creatures, exotic and mundane to us are also named.

Horses are not all that Elisha saw. He witnessed "chariots" as well. Angels can and do use vehicles in heaven. It follows that they must possess and use some degree of technology. Can you imagine what our greatest inventors might have come up with and made if they had never died? Angels cannot die, and they have existed before mankind. What other marvels might they use in heaven that we haven't even imagined?

Also, where there are horses, there must be food for them and for the angels as well. Oh, yes, God says that angels eat. When God liberated Israel from slavery in Egypt, he led them out across a harsh barren desert, the wilderness of Sinai. But he didn't let them starve on their journey. Even after they angered God to the point that he made them wander there for forty years until the last of those who had offended God had died of old age. He sent the entire nation "the corn of heaven," angel's food called "manna" (Ex. 16:14-31; Ps. 78:22-25).

God calls manna "the corn of heaven." Not *like*, it *is*. So what is corn? Corn is a grain, an edible seed plant cultivated for food. The angels grow and eat manna and other foods in heaven. The same as they raise and care for horses and other plants and animals. Other plants we know that they grow include flax for the linen clothing that at least some angels wear. For example, in Revelation we have: "and the seven angels came out of the temple, having the seven plagues, clothed in fine linen white and clean" (Rev. 15:6), and "the armies *which were* in heaven followed him upon white horses, clothed in fine linen white and clean" (Rev. 19:14). Other plants we know grow in heaven include a variety of spices. These include cassia, cinnamon, frankincense, galbanum, myrrh, onycha, stacte, sweet calamus, and several others. Fruiting plants in heaven include dates, olives, pomegranates, and more, as well as many other plants of all types.

Heaven must have an incredible diverse garden of wondrous plants to enjoy for a wide variety of purposes. One of the earliest terms used for God's heaven in the Bible is "paradise." The same word used to describe God's Garden of Eden in Genesis. God's personal garden, built for His personal enjoyment here on Earth, a reflection of His heaven above. There is probably a similar garden above that it resembled (see Is. 51:3).

Paradise is another term that was also commonly used for "Abraham's bosom," the temporary resting place within the earth where Lazarus went when he died in Luke 16:22. It's also what the apostle Paul reports he visited when he was stoned to death outside of Lystra on his second missionary journey (Acts 14:19): "How that he was caught up in to paradise, and heard unspeakable words, which it is not lawful for a man to utter" (II Cor. 12:4). Paul learned certain things while he was there, in Paradise, God forbade him to repeat here to us on Earth. It's not that Paul *couldn't* repeat it. God told told him *not* to repeat it, and went so far as to allow a fallen angel, one of satan's demons, to torment Paul on an ongoing basis for the rest of his time on Earth, as a gentle reminder that there were limits to what Paul was allowed to reveal to us as God's apostle, His personal messenger to mankind. Note also that Paul said he was "caught up" to the third heaven or paradise. Caught up, carried, much as the angels did with Lazarus. Clearly, some angels are tasked with the transport and delivery of souls outside their physical bodies. At least for those souls bound for paradise.

God built a paradise on earth, placed mankind there to cultivate it, much as angels likely cultivate a similar garden in the third heaven.

It is also of interest to note that in general, Christians are the only ones who refer to the realm of this third heaven as "Heaven." Although outsiders consider Islam and Judaism to be parallel or kindred belief systems, and both recognize this same concept of heaven, they both use the original term: paradise. A much more descriptive and better understood term, "paradise" is more helpful for us to understand and imagine what we should expect when we arrive there. Paradise is however professed to be different in those religions than it is for Christians. For example, Judaism promises its followers a paradise and everlasting life here on this earth. They also claim to follow and obey the same God. However, they ignore much of what God has told them about what He has done and is doing with mankind as a whole, including in regard to our current dispensation of grace. The promises they expect and anticipate apply to a different time period. They have also rejected large portions of their own sacred texts and prophecies and as a result have rejected Jesus as their Christ or Messiah. Most notable among some of these prophecies are: Is.53; Ps. 22;, Dan. 9:24-27; Jer. 31:31-34; and Prov. 30:4; all of which are present in God's completed Bible amongst and alongside hundreds of other scriptures identifying Jesus as the Christ. As a result, Judaism overlooks Jesus and awaits a messiah that is now thousands of years overdue according to their own scriptures. A messiah who lied about when he would come. Still, they wait. Their scriptures promise paradise on earth in a time yet to come and completely miss what God is doing now, which they never foresaw from their prophecies. At this time, all saved Jews and Gentiles alike go to the same eternal paradise, in heaven above. The only exceptions among those who die today, now, are those human souls bound for the eternal lake of fire.

Nonetheless, consider which sounds more promising, more tempting, more desirous, wherever it is located: "paradise," or "heaven"? Heaven is more ambiguous and could apply to vast empty spaces over our heads, nothing worth celebrating for most of us. Perhaps the modern Christian use of the word heaven to ascribe the resting place of Christian souls is another ploy by the Great Deceiver himself to mislead and discourage Christians from seeking greater rewards and pleasures above in favor of the inferior, temporary, tangible, immediate earthly temptations that are close at hand. Look at popular advertising. How many promise "heaven" in the experience that they promote? How many promise a taste or experience of "paradise"? It seems like the satan has done a great job reducing the appeal of heaven to mankind.

Another aspect to consider of this concept of God's mirrored gardens is the concept of soil or dirt, the very ground from which they grow. Plants require soil to grow here on Earth, the same as they do in paradise. This is further evidence that God fashioned this planet to resemble paradise in preparation for bringing His home and residence down to us on Earth. Similar plants have similar requirements for their soil.

Likewise, other features of this planet resemble those in Heaven above. There are mountains on earth, and there are mountains in paradise. Here's one example, a particular mountain the great deceiver covets from God: "thou hast said in thine heart, I will ascend into heaven, I will exalt my throne above the stars of God: I will sit also upon the mount of the congregation, in the sides of the north" (Is. 14:13). This passage makes clear that this mountain isn't found anywhere on Earth. This is a special mountain far above, where angels gather before God on a regular basis (see e.g. Job 1:6, 2:1). A throne sits on this mountain, one of the three thrones of God that the satan is dedicated to usurping for himself to prove that he, satan, is "like the Most High."

Another specific mount is mentioned in the book of Ezekiel, the "holy mountain of God," another heavenly mountain, upon which God receives regular worship from the angelic hosts. Before he sinned against God and fell from his place of extreme privilege Lucifer, now satan, "the adversary" of God, was "the anointed cherub that covereth" whose job, in part, was to lead these angelic hosts's worship of God - until he sought to wrest the dominion and that worship from God for himself. satan "wast upon the holy mountain God; thou hast walked up and down in the midst of the stones of fire" (Ez. 28:14). A mountain, quite possibly an active volcano, in paradise. It stands to reason that these special mountains are only two amongst many, as we on earth have many mountains but only one Everest, another replication of God's heavenly environment in His creation of planet Earth.

As there are mountains, and mountains are made of various types of stones and minerals, both are present both in heaven above and on earth below, thus we find another parallel. We mentioned earlier a few of those that we know for a fact exist in Paradise: gold, jasper, precious stones, and many other base minerals. Silica, the main component of glass, is in great abundance here on Earth. We saw it is present in God's own throne room. Sulfur is another mineral found in both environments.

Sulfur is a main component of the "brimstone" mentioned in the Bible. It rains down from heaven more than once to destroy God's enemies. For example: "Then the Lord rained upon Sodom and Gomorrah brimstone and fire from the Lord out of heaven" (Gen.19:24). And "I will rain upon him, and upon his bands, and upon the many people that are with him, an overflowing rain, and great hailstones, fire, and brimstone" (Ez. 38:22). Sulfur is found in abundance on Earth, and it will be a primary component of the "everlasting lake of fire," God's memorial to His enemies, their punishment, and His final victory over satan and all who followed satan and turned their backs on God's offer of eternal paradise (see Is. 66:24; Rev. 19:20; & 20:15). This will be an eternal display for all of creation to view and remember the price of rebellion against God. Obviously, this sulfurous brimstone can be found in both paradise and Earth. Both places have similar soils and ground as God designed and intended they should.

The surface of most of our planet is covered with water. There is also abundant water in various forms in God's paradise. Once again, this reflects God's intent to mirror His heaven on planet Earth. There is no shortage of scripture passages that illustrate this fact, even from the beginnings of Genesis, the account of Noah in Genesis seven, verses 11 through 12, and many, many more throughout the entire

Bible. Here's one unmistakable example: "Praise him ye heavens of heavens, and you waters that *be* above the heavens" (Ps. 148:4), which matches perfectly with the account of Genesis 1:7. The preceding verses in the Psalms passage all deal with angels, the stars, moon, and celestial heavens. There is no ambiguity to debate. There are abundant vast bodies of water in paradise.

Other earthly features God speaks of in His heaven above include clouds and rainbows, both closely associated with water as well as God's own presence. In paradise, as on Earth, these clouds soar far above the surface of the ground below. Satan mentions them when he challenges God for dominion over all creation in both heaven and earth: "I will ascend above the heights of the clouds; I will be like the most High" (Is. 14:14).

If you question whether satan refers to clouds in the skies of paradise or earth, consider that throughout the scriptures clouds are connected with God's presence. More than 100 times. They are closely associated with His holiness, accompany Him, and are a familiar sight to the angels in paradise as well as here.

On Earth, clouds and rainbows are connected. So to in paradise above. Consider the following reports of the prophet Ezekiel and apostle John: "And I saw as the color of amber, as the appearance of fire round about within it, from the appearance of his loins even upward, and from the appearance of his loins even downward, I saw as it were the appearance of fire, and it had brightness round about. As the appearance of the bow that is in the cloud in the day of rain, so *was* the appearance of the brightness round about. This *was* the appearance of the likeness of the glory of the Lord. And when I saw *it*, I fell on my face, and I heard a voice of one that spake" (Ez.1:27-18, also 8:2). "And he that sat was to look upon like a jasper and a sardine stone: and *there* was a rainbow round about the throne, in sight like unto an emerald" (Rev. 4:3). It is clear that rainbows are more than the symbol of God's promise to man to never again destroy the earth by flood. Rainbows are also an integral part of His appearance and a familiar sight in paradise.

All of which is fine and dandy, but why didn't God create something new and exotic for His second home? The short answer is that God intends Earth, specifically His custom city, to be His capital as well as His home. He will eventually bring together several disparate plans for mankind and His various creations into a single integrated cohesive whole, each part working in concert with all of the others and including angelic creations in distant ages to come, hinted at in Eph. 1:10. It is important to God that His most important creations are comfortable while they conduct business in His capital.

There will be nothing to impede our glorification of God in His presence.

If you still doubt God's design and intent to replicate paradise on this planet, consider God's directions for the construction of His temple and its implements of worship. Christ is described as the high priest for all of mankind: "we have such an high priest, who is set on the right hand of the throne of the Majesty in the heavens; a minister of the sanctuary, and of the true tabernacle, which the Lord pitched, and not man" (Heb.8:1-2). The "true tabernacle" being a temple to God in paradise that was supposed to be reflected on earth in Israel's tabernacle and temple. If God Himself pitched a tent, it was fastened to the ground. Being "in the heavens," there must be solid ground there, not a great sky blue void with shapeless drifting clouds. But God says more. He admonishes, or warns, Moses to "make all things according to the pattern shewed to thee." Why? God told Moses they were to be "the example and shadow of heavenly things," a reflection of what God erected in Paradise (Heb. 8:5). As God mirrored elements of Paradise in His creation of Earth, Moses was to emulate Him and copy the dimensions, structure, furnishings, and decorations of God's own "true tabernacle" above. God wants heaven and earth to match, paradise in both places. Further proof of this is also found in the recipes and instructions God gave Moses for His worship in this holy tabernacle.

These recipes and their instructions are found in Exodus chapter thirty; for "oil of holy anointment" in verses twenty-two through twenty-five, and spices for perfume to be burned as incense in verses thirty-four through thirty-seven. Note also God's additional admonishment in verse thirty-seven: "ye shall not make to yourselves according to the composition thereof: it shall be unto thee holy for the Lord" (Ex. 30:37). All of the ingredients grow here on planet Earth. But they are used also in God's heaven above: "and another angel came and stood at the altar, having a golden censer; and there was given unto him much incense, that he should offer *it* with the prayers of all saints upon the golden altar which was before the throne" (Rev. 8:3). The same as Moses was told to do in the earthly tabernacle below, in Exodus thirty verse thirty-six.

We haven't even touched on the presence of other precious metals and stones, musical instruments, woods, plants, trees, storehouses and what they contain, as well as books and many other items that God declares are present and always will be present in His Heaven, paradise. We've still seen enough to understand what God says and appreciate that He always wanted and intended this planet to closely resemble His original paradise. satan and the consequences of His rebellion are the reason that they don't.

PARADISE, OR RETIREMENT HOME?

We have established that Heaven and Earth look a lot alike because God always intended to dwell on Earth, but what do we have to look forward to if we go to paradise? What does everyone do for forever in paradise? What do they do now? Pop culture is full of sayings that suggest Heaven is boring, it's more fun or better to sin and party now.

Nothing could be farther from the truth.

If you've ever gone on too long a vacation - yes, there is such a thing - then you already know that any place, no matter how pleasant, can become boring after a time. God designed us to work, to act on His other creations. We have assigned duties or tasks, and so do the angels. We need those activities to remain healthy. All of which suggests that for paradise to be ideal, there must be activities. But what are they?

Angels receive commandments from the Lord. They do God's will, as He instructs: "Bless the Lord, ye his angels, that excel in strength, that do his commandments, hearkening unto the voice of his word. Bless ye the Lord, all *ye* his hosts; *ye* ministers of his, that do his pleasure" (Ps. 103:20-21). So will we. God won't let us sit idle, grow bored, or become discontent in paradise. God promises there will be plenty of work and entertainment activities to keep us busy, *forever.* And we won't be under- or over-worked either. We will truly enjoy what we do.

As for specifics, almost everything the Bible discloses about angels's activities in heaven is related to God's program with Israel and doesn't apply to us today - including promises of their personal protection. God isn't focused on Israel right now. We know the angels are learning something special God wants them, and perhaps us as well, to understand by being "hands off" and watching us and our use and reliance upon the Holy Spirit. But they also have day to day lives to live, and that includes a number of routine ongoing activities from which we can infer with confidence many of their other activities now and into the future.

While angels watch and learn from our behavior, someone tends to God's garden above. Manna and other crops are grown, tended, and harvested for the needs of the angelic hosts. The archangel Michael leads and prepares the incredible angelic armies until Christ assumes command of them for the final battles against satan and his followers. All armies drill, train, and prepare for combat. They also need to repair and maintain any equipment and supplies that they will need. We know this vast army includes horses, which require attention, care, and exercise as well. In addition to the routine martial activities of a standing army, athletic sports no doubt abound as well.

Evidence of angelic sports can be found in the Bible as early as Genesis. Abraham's grandson Jacob was renowned as a very strong man in a time when some of mankind grew to enormous proportions; some as large as twelve and thirteen feet tall (see e.g. Gen. 6:4 & many others). The Smithsonian Museum in Washington D.C. today has a sub- basement with entire vast rooms full of the preserved skeletons of some of these giant humans recovered from burial sites, coal veins, and other sites from all around the world. Jacob himself was so strong that he challenged an angel to wrestle when they argued.

Then, as now, wrestling was recognized as a sport with specified rules. In Genesis thirty-two verses twenty-four through thirty-two we see that Jacob wrestled that unnamed angel to a draw, even though most angels are far superior to most humans in most respects. Neither

Jacob nor this unnamed angel was able to win the match. But this angel knew the rules of the sport. From this we can infer and expect to see wrestling and other olympic style sports in paradise. Some of our own sports may have originated there. After all, the original Olympics were held in honor of false gods, some of whom no doubt were angels or their half-human descendants whom ancient legends say taught men these sports and other activities to begin with. It seems very safe to say that there will be sports in heaven. And where there are sports, there are always spectators.

Angels transport the souls of dead saints to paradise when their bodies die as we saw with Lazarus and the apostle Paul earlier. Today they are transported up into God's own presence in the third heaven above, as they have since Christ's triumph at the cross. There the saints socialize and await their resurrection bodies and new duties. Now, the only souls that descend into the earth when their bodies die go to wait in Hades, Torments, "hell," until their time of judgment before Christ.

No doubt angels engage in fashioning clothing, equipment, tools, other items, or even inventing new technologies to assist with various activities, while other angels cook and prepare foods, care for various animals, entertain others, and perform other common daily activities. By no means is this an extensive list of angelic activities, only some of the more apparent ones. Even in paradise, there is always plenty of activity for everyone to stay busy. Especially in view of the promise to us of heavenly government in 1 Timothy 2:12.

In the book of Zechariah, we learn that all the nations of the earth will be required to come and present themselves before the Lord in an appointed weeklong festival, the Feast of Tabernacles (Zechariah 14:16). The angels already do. Even satan comes to these gatherings to give account of their activities to the Lord: "Now there was a day when the sons of God came to present themselves before the Lord, and satan came also among them. And the Lord said unto satan, whence comest thou? Then satan answered the Lord, and said, from going to and fro in the earth, and from walking up and down in it (Job 1:6-7). And "again there was a day when the sons of God came to present themselves before the Lord, and satan came also among them to present himself before the Lord" (Job 2:1). These regular meetings probably occur before the "mount of the congregation" we discussed earlier, much as they will on earth before the new mountain God will raise beside Jerusalem (See Is. 2:2-3; Ez.40:2,43:12; & others).

As for the specific activities of the dead in Christ *right now*, the Bible gives us no specifics while they await their new bodies except that they are now in God's presence, probably in His throne room above. We do know that they are aware of their surroundings, the presence of others, and can communicate with others, all from the accounts of Paul and Lazarus. We also know that they are not bored while they wait, but this fact requires understanding another concept.

PERFECT TIME . . .

Now let us take a look at a more esoteric but critical concept: What Time Looks Like in Heaven, and how that affects our experience of paradise.

The experience of time is an integral part of life, even life everlasting. It is part of creation. it is unavoidable. But what exactly is Time, and why does it matter? Simply put, time is a continual progression of events, one event succeeding another. Our experience of that phenomenon is what we refer to as "time." Time is inseparable from eternity as eternity is an unending continuous succession or progression of sequential events. Time is therefore integral to what God is doing and helps to define His creation.

The concept of time and our unending experience of events are inseparable from our existence, both here and in paradise. There is a difference in our experience of time in paradise from what we experience now. In paradise, there is no sin, so there is nothing to corrupt and distort our experience of time. Satan and sin do not control the experience and our perception of time there.

Right now, all of creation, Earth, and our known universe included, is scarred by the effects of sin. These effects are well illustrated by mechanical clock or watch's winding down. Modern science refers to this effect as entropy. It is a result of sin, First satan's and later the other angels's, as well as mankind's subsequent disobedience and rebellion against God and His original design. Entropy itself is an effect a symptom, of the "bondage of corruption" that all of creation suffers under as a result of being "subject to [satan's] vanity" (Rom 8:20-22). It is also proof of sin's entrance into the world (Rom. 5:12).

God's purpose in creation continues, but for the time being all of creation remains under satan's controlling influence, displaying his inferior capability to maintain this universe and all within it. And it will remain under satan and sin's influence until Christ's promised return to claim his rightful rulership. The effects of sin, its "bondage of corruption," and God's condemnation of the same have scarred and effaced all creation, including Earth, reduced its capabilities and function, and marred its designed glory into something less than what God created, desires, and intends. This corrupting influence produces drastic effects on our very experience of all events within that creation. These cumulative effects are the burden of time that oppresses many of us today. Ennui is our experience of this very burden.

God's Heaven, Paradise, is outside that corruption and its influence. The very experience of all those now in God's presence is different from our own as a result. When we enter Paradise, we don't step outside of time and time itself is not altered. But our perception of time does change. Sin's corrupting influence and the resulting burden we experience is removed.

The burden of time we experience on earth takes its toll on us in several ways. It tires us. It wears us down. We grow weak and decay, the very definition of entropy. We notice these effects compound over time and call this aging or growing old. We notice them affect our mind as well as our bodies in both the short and long term. We grow weary. Events can occur too fast for our weary minds to process, leading us to feel frustrated, overwhelmed, unable to cope. Time seems to drag on and on. We may wonder if an unpleasant situation will ever end, while more joyous events seem to fly by us too fast to enjoy in full. Boredom and impatience are less extreme versions of these same effects, all part of the "bondage of corruption" that satan has brought upon all of creation and our experience of it, which is the very essence of the concept of time.

Happy and joyous events are also affected by this burden of time that we experience today. We lament when they seem to fly by. We feel deprived of sufficient time to enjoy them. We mourn the adage "all good things must come to an end." We want these pleasant experiences to continue and never end. All tangible effects of the burden of time on us while under satan's dominion.

Now imagine life without any of these perceptions affecting us. Hard, isn't it? But that's how our experience of time will be in paradise. Go ahead, take a little while and really think about it before you continue this study.

Time isn't the problem. The *burden* of time is. A result of satan's extreme arrogance and vanity that has been imposed on all of creation, itself a side effect of satan's temporary rulership. When that relationship ends and Christ's reign begins, this burden of time, along with all the other effects of satan's bondage of corruption will be removed, an event that all of creation looks forward to, as seen in Romans 8:19,21.

In paradise our experience of time will be as God designed and intended it. The burden ceases to exist. Time will no longer oppress us. Time, and all our experiences and activities once again glorify God and His goals and efforts, not satan's shortcomings.

God is never bored or impatient, like we often are for His return, or even for lesser events. Time doesn't drag by or rush past God or those with him in Paradise. The perception of time in Paradise is undistorted by the corruption of sin that we now endure here on Earth.

Consider what the apostle Paul shares with us regarding future time: "now unto him that is able to do exceedingly abundantly above all that we ask or think, according to the power that worketh in us, unto him *be* glory in the church by Christ Jesus throughout all ages, world without end. Amen" (Eph. 3:20-21). Paul is concluding his prayer with his recognition of how time is meant to be anticipated. Paul isn't begging for help to endure another day's troubles, he is giving thanks and recognition of God's idea of eternity: an ongoing procession of ages. Long successive spans of time with significant distinctions that together comprise "eternity." An unceasing continuance of experiences in a "world without end." In our current state, this is a very oppressive, even overwhelming concept, but it isn't to Paul. Paul recognizes the different experience of time's passage in paradise. He knows and understands from being there himself that time itself is no longer significant, only a milestone that signifies completion of a particular goal or stage of God's ongoing plan. God's eternal unending plan. Plans that continue forever.

At present we are so burdened by time and the brevity of our current existence that this concept may well be staggering, maybe even incomprehensible to many of us. But Paul has been in Paradise, experienced it, and returned to tell us. He knows what God says He is doing, as should we. God has a plan for us with ongoing goals and accomplishments, new experiences to look forward to, forever.

Paul glorified God in his prayer, even as he gave things in recognition of God's eternal design and plan. This is exactly what God desires and intended. God wants the glory and He wants to receive it from us forever. In return, God promises us unimaginable rewards, wealth, and comfort beyond anything we can imagine, all in exchange for our worship and glorification of Him (Is. 64:4; I Cor. 2:9). All of creation, glorifying God in thanks and worship forever is God's desire.

Paul refers to God the "Father of glory" in Ephesians 1:17. Part of His purpose in both sending and sacrificing His own Son, our Lord Jesus Christ, to redeem us from sin's corrupting influence and satan's rebellious attempt to usurp rulership of all God's creation is to encourage us to thank and glorify Him and Him alone, forever, for all of eternity.

Time, the events and our experiences of them that comprise time, our appreciation of them, and of time itself, is all meant to glorify God and provide more opportunities and reasons to do so. God wants us to thank Him and to do so unburdened. Even now, the burden of time has been removed from everyone present before Him in heaven. They already experience the *glory* of time as God designed it rather than its burden. Each moment, each experience is grand, something enjoyed and cherished. Boredom, impatience, ennui, fatigue, pain, and sorrow do not exist in paradise. There is nothing there to distract or detract from our enjoyment of each moment, each experience, as much, or more than all of those that came before it.

Satan's bondage and burdens cease to exist in Paradise. Our capacity for pleasure, for enjoyment, will be limitless. It should be a great comfort and source of joy to us to recognize and remember these facts when we think about loved ones who have preceded us to paradise in God's presence.

Until the time that we join them, there is something more for us to understand about our time here on Earth. Here and now, the hands of every clock are shears, trimming each of us away, piece by piece, bit by bit, until we implode from this very burden. Yet while we live and remain physically present in this "evil world," those of us who are saints in Christ can in fact bring God honor and glory now, before all of creation as beings "created in Christ Jesus unto good works." Paul reminds us of this fact, and that we can overcome satan's burden of time here and now, thru the power provided by the Holy Spirit when he says, "see then that ye walk circumspectly, not as fools, but as wise, redeeming the time, because the days are evil. Wherefore, be ye not unwise, but understanding what the will of the Lord *is*" (Eph. 5:15-17).

Our sanctified position "in Christ Jesus" gives us the capacity to glorify God and His plan *right now.* We don't have to wait for paradise and removal of the curses sin and satan burden us with now. God empowers us to live according to His plan and in doing so glorify Him for all to see. This doesn't mean our burden of time will cease to exist while we yet live. Like all the rest of creation we will still endure the "bondage of corruption" while in this physical body. What it does mean is that our time here doesn't have to dishonor God. We don't have to honor satan, the bondage and burdens his corruption and evil have brought upon God's creation. We don't have to promote or encourage satan's self-destructive agenda.

Even modern physicists agree that this universe and all creation's inevitable outcome on its current course is complete destruction. And they only recognize the effects we've already discussed, not their true cause or origin. The only possible outcome of satan's program of evil is the total destruction and dissolution of all he seeks to rule. We have the opportunity to counteract some of satan's influence and thereby help liberate creation, provide it the liberty to also glorify God now, by living in accord with God's design now, *despite* the corrupting and evil influences of satan that surround and seek to suffocate us, all by simply obeying God's Word, now, in this life, on Earth.

Understanding that we have such a tremendous opportunity and privilege here today can also have a great mollifying effect on our personal burden of time while here on Earth. We don't share that burden or its effects, but we can greatly reduce their impact on our lives. It should also make us realize that there can be no greater waste of time for a Christian than to continue living hand in hand in "fellowship with the unfruitful works of darkness" under satan's program for this world. Not to mention the future eternal rewards we'd miss out on for failing to obey God and service as His willing ambassadors, on display for all to see what God expects of mankind in this present evil world.

OUR GLORIOUS NEW BODY

While we do not have a detailed scientific understanding of the mechanics, God has provided us confidence in our eternal future. We remain unique individuals. We remain recognizable to those who knew us here on Earth. We are not absorbed into another entity. We do not lose our distinct identity. We can recognize and sense our surroundings as well as interact and socialize with others nearby. Even before we receive our new bodies.

We have the accounts of Paul and Lazarus that illustrate all of these facts and more in Luke chapter sixteen for Lazarus and II Corinthians chapter twelve for Paul. Paul was unable to tell whether or not he was present in his body while in paradise. We have another unique example, the only person who has already been resurrected as promised (I Cor. 15:20). Every single man, woman, and child who God gives a living soul will eventually receive their own resurrection body. But there will be more than one kind of resurrection body, with different capabilities and purposes (see e.g. Dan. 12:2; John 5:29; & I

Cor. 15:38-42). As this study is on heaven, we will only focus on the body designed for heaven.

The privilege of living in paradise forever requires a living body. None of us will live there in our current body, which was designed to rely on ties to Earth's environment that also prevent it from functioning for long away from Earth. We need a new body with different capabilities.

For the time being, most of God's future blessings in paradise remain hidden to us (I Cor. 2:9). We do have a lot of information about this body we will receive, but there is probably more about it that we won't know until we have it than that we know from scripture. But we are given Christ's own resurrected body as an example of what we can expect from it.

Among the details we do know are that it will be very similar to Christ's own (I Cor. 15:20,23). It is free of sin's influence and so it is immortal; able to function and exist in the celestial realm, is not restricted to the earth; and each is to some degree unique (I Cor. 15:35-58). We know it can eat and enjoy food (Luke 24:42-43). We also know that it is capable of feats of speed of travel that defy our current senses and understanding of the known rules of physics (e.g. Luke 24:32). It is compared in many ways to the stars in the sky.

Throughout Scripture, God's holy presence is revealed amidst bright light. We saw Him clothe himself with light in Psalms 104:2. He appeared to Moses shining with His glory on Mount Sinai in Exodus 33:18-23. That brief exposure to the least portion of God's presence had a lasting effect on Moses: "when he came down from the mount, that Moses wist not that the skin of his face shone; ...and all the children of Israel saw Moses, behold, the skin of his face shown... *till* Moses had done speaking with them, he put a veil upon his face" (Ex. 34:29-30,33). "The children of Israel could not steadfastly behold the face of Moses for the glory of his countenance" (II Cor. 3:7).

Other passages declare that God's glory shines forth from Him as well. Daniel 12:3 reveals that in our new bodies, we too will "shine" with a reflection of God's own glory, commensurate to our faithfulness to Him in this life, forever, as indicated in the comparison given in I Corinthians 15:41. Christ's appearance in his own resurrection body confirms this in Revelation 1:16. One of the characteristics of these new bodies is their visible reflection of God's own glory, which our current bodies lack.

As members of the new "body of Christ" God is building of us, we are promised to share in all aspects of Christ's resurrection. Other passages that document this reflection of God's glory in our new body include Romans 8:17-23; I Corinthians 15:40-42; II Corinthians 3:7-

11,18; and Colossians 3:4. As often as this feature of our new bodies is mentioned there must be a great significance attached to this aspect of our resurrection body. In Ephesians, we learn not only that we will reside and function in the heavens (Eph.2:6; also Phil. 3:20), we will also replace those condemned fallen angelic rulers who follow satan and his rebellion against God (see I Cor. 6:3). Clearly, for us to serve such a function, our new bodies must be capable of going wherever these angelic creatures can go.

We have reviewed but a very few of the great many nuggets of information God has provided to us in scripture about what awaits us in paradise. Understanding even this little bit of what paradise, heaven if you prefer, will be like should make a thrilling impact on our immortal souls and encourage us in the toils of this life. We should be able to appreciate what awaits us when we anticipate death and eternity, or think of loved ones who've gone ahead of us to join our Lord and Savior in heaven. Marvelous glory and splendor exists there and we should know at least a little of what we have to look forward to when we join them.

The glory and grandeur of God's prepared paradise far exceeds all we see or perceive now on this planet, but it won't all be foreign to us. Earth was modeled after God's own wondrous heaven and paradise to fulfill His plan and purpose with all of creation. Our existence here gives us only the barest glimpse of the true majesty of the appearance, environment, and activities that we will enjoy in paradise.

I hope, my friend and neighbor, that I will see you there.

WHERE ARE YOU GOING WHEN YOU DIE?

We saved the most important question you can ask about Heaven for last. Perhaps our brief glimpse into what to expect we'll help you decide whether or not you want to spend your eternal existence in paradise or not. The only alternative to God's prepared Paradise is His everlasting lake of fire, often termed hell. This decision is yours and yours alone. It always has been.

Are *you* going to heaven when you die and leave planet Earth behind?

Not sure yet, or are you not ready to decide? Then let's rephrase the question: *If you die in the next five minutes, will you be present with God in paradise, . . . or not?*

"Yes" or "no."

There is no other possible answer.

If you can't answer "yes" without any hesitation whatsoever, or have the slightest doubt whatsoever, ask yourself another question, and go find the answer.

Now.

Nothing else could ever be more important. Some of us don't have five minutes left to live. More than 150,000 people leave this life every single day. You don't know when you will be one of them.

Here's what God says is the answer to knowing that you will go to Paradise as soon as you die. Through the apostle Paul, God declares that He offers salvation to all who believe "the gospel of Christ." "I'm not ashamed of the gospel of Christ: for it is the power of God unto salvation to everyone that believeth: to the Jew first, and also to the Greek. For therein is the righteousness of God revealed from faith to faith: as it is written, the just shall live by faith" (Rom. 1:16-17). This is the only way today that God will spare you from the penalty of your own sins, what Christians commonly refer to as "being saved" from the everlasting lake of fire and its unending tortures, some of which are glimpsed in Isaiah 66:24; Rev. 20:10,15; & 21:8.

Not everyone will choose paradise for their eternal home. There will always be some people who reject God's gifts and promises, including salvation, and others who don't believe. Scripture addresses all of their arguments and justifications and says they are all without any merit. Still more are deceived by satan and his allies on a regular basis, some into believing false gospels with conditions, promises, or requirements that God never gave. Yet more don't understand the gospel message, simple as it is. The Bible addresses this to: "the preaching of the cross is to them that perish foolishness" (I Cor 1:18) and "if our gospel be hid, it is hid to them that are lost" (II Cor. 4:3). Another broader passage encompasses these, but it can also apply to Christians in that if you don't need to know, it isn't guaranteed that the Holy Spirit will 'reveal all' to you simply because you open the book and read a scripture. Failure to appreciate this concept is a primary cause for the myriad sects and divisions among supposed Christians today, and the foundation of every single denomination: "the natural man receiveth not the things of the Spirit of God: for they are foolishness unto him: neither can he know *them*, because they're spiritually discerned" (I Cor. 2:14). No man can properly and fully interpret the Word of God without the Holy Spirit, and He gives to whom He deems necessary, as He desires. It's as simple as that.

Do *you* need to be saved from the price of your own sins? Well, stop and think. Ask yourself, have you ever done any of the following: lie (even a 'little white' one, they count too), steal (borrowing without permission counts), cheat, hate, or lust (for food, power, money, or sex perhaps)? Ever envy someone else's good fortune, property, or spouse? Of course you have, we all have. Ever think that you are too nice or too good to go to hell? That is pride, another sin. God says, "There is none righteous, no, not one" (Rom. 3:10; also Ps.14:3; Is. 64:6). God is the one who decides if you go to heaven and He has already given us His decision: on your own, no one goes.

Not one of us is good enough to go to Paradise on our own merit. "The heart [of mankind] *is* deceitful above all *things*, and desperately wicked" (Jeremiah 17:9). These are the main points of the entire Old Testament. The Jews believe that they can somehow earn their salvation, their "ticket to paradise." That is the entire point of following the Mosaic law. But they can't. No one can (Rom. 3:19-20, 9:31, 10:5). We *need* God's help. And why not, He created us unable to achieve this perfection on our own, so it is only fair if He also helps us out of this problem. That is why God, in His abounding love for all of mankind, sacrificed Himself, as Jesus Christ, on the altar of His own need for perfect justice to pay the price for all the sins we cannot pay for ourselves. The ultimate act of His recognition of our limitations, His perfect love, and forgiveness of our disobedience to Him.

Sin is nothing more or less than disobedience to God. Odds are that you have disobeyed God more than a few times. Mother Teresa did. Gandhi was a confessed murderer, and so was the apostle Paul - himself a prolific serial killer and mass murderer. How do you compare to them? if they weren't "good enough," neither are you.

Here is who the Bible says needs God's salvation, His forgiveness of sins: "the wrath of God is revealed from heaven against all ungodliness and unrighteousness of men" (Romans 1:18). That covers every last one of us. Every single one. No exceptions. That includes you. We are all "by nature the children of wrath." The wrath of God is what our deeds deserve. You need God's salvation. We all do.

Our natural tendency is to think we can somehow escape God's wrath on our own merit, or by relying on God's perfect love and patience with mankind. There is one problem with that idea. God is pure perfect love, but He is also pure perfect justice. And justice requires acknowledgement, recognition, and payment for every disobedient act, every sin against God's perfect design. A penalty *must* be paid to resolve every such debt, no matter what else you may have done. This is the message or the entire first chapter of the book of Romans. The second chapter addresses our natural tendencies: "thinkest thou this, O man that judgest them which do such things, and doest the same, that thou shalt escape the judgment of God?" (Rom. 2:3). That *is* exactly what most of us think, isn't it?

God tells us that very thought is pride; arrogance, another sin. We cannot escape God's judgment as we want to believe. The "wrath of God" is what we _will_ receive on our own merit. All of us. Every single one.

No attempt to improve yourself, no matter how sincere, will work, no matter how hard you try. You can't "make up" for even your own sins. No good works can offset them. They'll never balance. Every single moment of your entire life, from birth to death, would have to be continuous uninterrupted good works and obedience to every word from God to satisfy God's justice, if you were to earn your own salvation. You could never sin, never commit the smallest evil or offense whatsoever - not even once. You know full well you have not and never could do this. Paul says it's not even humanly possible: "now we know that what things soever the law saith it saith to them who are under the law: that every mouth may be stopped, and all the world may become guilty before God. Therefore, by the deeds of the law there shall no flesh be justified in His sight: for by the law *is* the knowledge of sin" (Rom. 3:19-20). "The law" refers to the same Mosaic Law that God gave to the nation of Israel when they swore that they could and would obey any rule or law that He gave them, intending to prove their own worth, or self-righteousness, to God. They believed they were sufficient to earn paradise for themselves, and many of them still do. They couldn't. They have all failed. Every last one who has tried.

All mankind, even including you, is "guilty before God." Guilty, deserving wrathful punishment for our disobedience and unable to do anything about it. "For the wages of sin *is* death" (Rom. 6:23a). Worse yet, there's more: "that they all might be damned who believed not the truth, but had pleasure in unrighteousness" (I Thes.2:12).

That's not good news, it's terrible news! The gospel is supposed to be good news, right? Okay, here is the good news: You can't do it, but God already has. His act of perfect Love appeased His need for perfect justice. Instead of an entire life of perfect obedience, we only need a single perfect act of obedience to clear our way to paradise: belief in our Lord Jesus Christ with acceptance of God's gift.

God says that He created us in our weaknesses and imperfections, but He also gave us a way out: "the gift of God is eternal life through Jesus Christ our Lord" (Rom. 6:23b). "Christ died for our sins according to the scriptures; and that he was buried, and that he rose again the third day according to the scriptures" (I Cor. 15:3-4). This is "the righteousness of God without the law."

Paul's full explanation of God's salvation message is a bit longer but amounts to the same thing: "the righteousness of God without the law is manifested, being witnessed by the law and the prophets; even the righteousness of God *which* is by faith of Jesus Christ unto all and upon all of them that believe: for there is no difference: for all have sinned, and come short of the glory of God; being justified freely by his grace through the redemption that is in Christ Jesus: whom God hath set forth *to be* a propitiation through faith in his blood, to declare his righteousness for the remission of sins that are past, through the forbearance of God; to declare, *I say,* at this time his righteousness: that he might be just, and the justifier of him which believeth in Jesus" (Rom. 3:21-26).

What you can't do for yourself, God has done for you by and through the Lord Jesus Christ, part of God incarnate in our condemned world. Christ substituted himself, took upon himself the debt and penalty for all of our sins, and offered himself before God as a blood sacrifice for each and every one of us, an ultimate act of love (see e.g. Eph.5:3; 1 Tim. 2:6).

That someone who didn't deserve punishment at all paid our debt of his own volition satisfied God's sense of justice. Someone had to pay the price for all of our disobedience and Christ did. That is "propitiation": complete forgiveness of our sin debts for all of our disobedience to God. All Christ expects in return is your recognition and acceptance of this fact as your sole qualification to get into heaven.

Acceptance of Christ's sacrifice and death for you on the cross, to pay for your sins, is your "justification," your right to enter paradise with God forever.

After Christ's willing self-sacrifice was complete, his work finished, God raised Christ from the dead, a symbol of what awaits us if we recognize and accept God's freely offered gift of salvation.

Imagine the greatest blockbuster entertainment event ever. A single ticket costs more than you can ever afford. It costs more than a VIP seat at every event, venue, and every performance in your entire lifetime. Christ's self-sacrifice reserved and paid for your ticket. It's in your name at God's box office, waiting for you to pick it up. That ticket has your name on it and the box office staff know you in person. All you have to do is come by and pick it up and you go to the show. But you have to claim it before the show begins. There's no late admission allowed. This show begins the moment your body dies and you're soul leaves it behind.

All you have to do is believe: "if thou shalt confess with thy mouth the Lord Jesus, and shalt believe in thine heart that God hath raised him from the dead, thou shalt be saved" (Rom. 10:9).

What if you don't? What if you die before you make this choice? Will the box office staff come find you and force you to attend the celebration? Of course not! The choice is yours whether you attend, and yours alone. Join us in paradise if you want. Or go catch the only event you can afford on your own. The box office closes. God's staff goes home. Will you?

God did all the work, told you, and offered you a free ticket to paradise. He won't force it on you. Neither will I. God told you what He's done, why you need it, and how do you accept His invitation to the biggest party there will ever be. You do want to join us there in paradise don't you?

Pick up God's gift, His free ticket to paradise, in the privacy of your own soul before it is too late. God says to "believe in Jesus." That means you exclusively trust Jesus, you depend and rely on him and him alone and what he's done, and not on anything you can ever do.

You place your complete trust in his self-sacrifice on the cross for your salvation from satan's kingdom and eternity in the lake of fire.

If you believe, God will forgive you every sin you ever commit, no exceptions. Past, present, and future, you will be debt free with God. When you die, you will be transported to paradise with God. The only unpardonable sin in this dispensation of grace is rejecting Christ and his work on the cross for your salvation from eternity in the lake of fire. Let no one tell you otherwise.

Until the end of this dispensation and the end of the tribulation that follows, we still live under satan's rule while on earth, but we are no longer members of satan's kingdom. We are citizens of heaven. God's wrath, "Hell," and the lake of fire will never concern or trouble you again. You can never lose citizenship in heaven once you accept it. Scripture says: "being justified by faith, we have peace with God through our Lord Jesus Christ: by whom also we have access by faith into this grace wherein we stand, and rejoice in hope of the glory of God" (Rom.5:1-2). That grace is our salvation from satan's kingdom and future, our hope of eternal paradise.

Your soul's future is settled. You have complete control of that future, even beyond your body's death. You can never lose your "ticket" to paradise or miss you're ride there. Your "ticket" becomes a part of you, and we all die.

This is the greatest gift you can ever receive. Paul says: "by grace are ye saved through faith; and that not of yourselves: *it is* the gift of God: not of works, lest any man should boast" (Eph. 2:8-9), and: "thanks *be* unto God for His unspeakable gift" (II Cor.9:15). Paradise itself is just the beginning. Remember, God has a great many more gifts awaiting us when we get to heaven.

Belief is the only issue that decides your eternal home. What you pray in the privacy of your own soul is up to you. It is a reflection, a symbol of your belief, and that belief is what God says matters to Him.

What *do you* believe?

A Final Note From the Narrator

I hope one day to see and meet you in Paradise. In the meantime, I hope you enjoyed and benefit from this very brief study of Heaven. There is a lot more for you to discover and enjoy from God's Word to help you through your days here on Earth. I hope and encourage you to read and explore the rest of God's scriptures. As long as I am able, I welcome you to write me with your questions or feedback, or consider one of these other ministries for more information. Their information follows.

I also want to offer special thanks, not only to our Lord Jesus Christ, who made all of this possible in the first place, but also to the following ministries and resources. Each of these, and others besides, have helped me prepare and present this study to you. We only scratched the surface of this topic. There's so much more to learn and enjoy.

And may God bless you and your households my brethren, and all of the following who in some part provided assistance in the development and formation of this study, among others:

www.biblegateway.com, Enjoy the Bible Ministries |
www.enjoythebible.org & Keith Blades, www.helpersofyourjoy.com |
Berean Bible Ministries, Millennium Bible Institute | graceage.org,
www.trianglebiblechurch.org, www.shorewoodbiblechurch.org |
Rick Jordan, Southwest Bible Fellowship | www.butnow.org | Rick
Jordan Jr., & all our fellow departed brethren now awaiting our
arrival.

fecit 2021, A. Obtenebrix, begun Nov. 14, 2019.

Enjoyed this brief study and want more? Look for these upcoming works, available wherever fine books are sold in either print or digital format. Feel free to ask your favorite bookseller to request it, all titles are available from their distributors:

BIBLE ECONOMICS & PERSONAL FINANCE 101 – A Primer on the Biblical Principles of Acquiring & Maintaining Wealth

ARE WE THERE YET? – A Biblical Examination of the End Times Prophecies